Good Wins

Thomas Spriggs

ISBN: 9781794433922

DEDICATION

To those Fighting the Good Fight all around the World.
May God be with you in all your efforts.

CONTENTS

ACKNOWLEDGMENTS

To the man desperately undressing in the middle of the
Belgian forest in the middle of winter in 1944. I have
missed you all these years.

And to all the great men in the world.

FORWARD

Like many of you, I was delighted to discover Jordan Peterson at the beginning of 2018. His honesty and understanding of the realities of human nature and his criticism of postmodernism has been an exciting and amazing development, and I was inspired by him to write these books. For that, I am forever grateful.

I once promised to some of my friends about ten years ago I would write a book on hope. After a long period in which I have learned much about the subject here it is, strangely enough. It's not like I envisioned it, but I believe it is needful in these times.

This book is the companion to Mere Animals, where I discuss the corrupt beliefs of postmodernism and the horrible danger it is creating for the future of the world. The next 30-50 years will be one of the most critical in human history. This book is meant to be an antidote to the poison of this anti-Western philosophy that has polluted the world.

I was inspired by Mr. Peterson to finally put words to paper, but in truth, these books go back a lot farther than that in my thought. The genesis of my thinking on postmodernism started when I was working at a prior job.

I became friends with a young man, about 30 years old at the time. He was married and had a couple of children and seemed to have a decent life. On the surface, he was off to a great start, and had much to look forward to in the future.

The only issue was he did not see it that way. He looked to the future with a certain amount of dread, and believed his life would get worse, not better. He had no ambition, not even looking at better positions at that employer where we worked. He stated he would be perfectly happy just doing the job he had at the time until he could retire.

Whatever free time he had was spent either playing video games or watching Twitch or YouTube streams of others playing. And he was absolutely immovable in his attitude. He did not know when or how it would all go south, but he was certain it would. And he saw no hope we could find our way out.

He was just one in a innumerable collection of victims of the postmodernist assault on Western values and everyday people. It is a great picture of just how deeply the poison of postmodern beliefs have seeped into the body politic all over Westernized society. This is the root of our hopelessness and our opioid crisis that has devastated our society.

It is the natural response for a person who believes that all white men are automatically bad, that society is made up solely of the oppressed and oppressor. That the future belongs to communists and those who only goal is to seek revenge on those who set them up as equals. It is the natural result of an unending war on people of faith and traditional values.

It is possible to fight back against the corrupting force of the Hard Left and the New Atheism that has taken the levers of power in society. But we need a philosophy that points us in a new direction, that gives us a road map to better understanding our role in society. Then we can react correctly for those who would keep us in chains if they could.

Winning the war against our enemies on the Hard Left will not be easy; postmodernists are committed ideologues determined to overthrow western civilization and replace it with their own all-powerful state designed to control all public human behavior. They are not interested in whether people "come together" voluntarily or at the barrel of a gun, they are only interested in forcing standards of public behavior on us, the way the Soviet Union did before it fell and the Chinese do today. They are destroying the fabric of personal and cultural standards of millions of people all around the world.

The Muslims are likewise determined to impose sharia law all around the world. The populist belief in Islam is that of a worldwide caliphate covering the whole globe. As Islam has recovered from having been conquered by the Mongols and then the West, it has regained it's aggressive and expansionary drive. Postmodernism is the stumbling block keeping us from defending ourselves.

Fortunately, there is an answer; a real commitment to doing real good, for our families, our communities, and our nation. I believe it is possible to regain our cultural and social footing and secure the future of the planet. It's a long shot, one in a million, but I believe it is possible. And if you will believe with me, we may yet pull it off.

INTRODUCTION:
THE ONE THING

It is a strange and difficult thing to introduce yourself to the world through books. They tell you almost nothing provable about my habits, my character, or my motivations. You neither see me at my best nor at my worst. Reading a book requires stretching human capacity for imagination to the limit. You must trust a stranger with your heart and mind. It is a sharp sword, that has brought us in recent history genocide and war, yet also peace and prosperity. Reading and writing are not endeavors to be taken lightly.

So let me begin by saying that all I am writing in this peace, along with it's companion, Mere Animals, I do so for only one good reason; your best interests. I do have one redeeming quality, that I see it as my duty to pass what little I have learned in my 55 years on this small planet to the next generation. My earnest hope is to give you a fighting chance against the long odds you face.

It is not all sunshine and unicorn droppings; as I have

laid out in Mere Animals, we live in a time when we have too much power to indulge our iniquities, and not enough character to search for wholeness. I have seen silly videos of a man who looks upon people with compassion, unspeaking, until he somehow reaches them in a way their own children cannot. Perhaps reading a book is not nearly as fraught with crazy possibilities as I thought.

Since I was able to share the darker side of our current predicament, allow me now to entertain to you a much happier idea; that all is not yet lost, that we need not slumber beneath the spell of meaninglessness, that there is a hope and a future should we agree to pursue it. And yet, I am going to put this into different terms than those who wish you to merely think positively, for thinking positive thoughts does not guarantee an outcome. If it did, we would suffer no economic downturns ever. If positive thought alone brought good, as others have pointed out, we would all be thin, rich, and happy.

The shallow and bitter water of temporary happiness cannot un-poison the soul, and usually adds to it. Despite the proclamations of a certain artist of somewhat limited ability, happiness is certainly not "the truth". If it were, why are so may so miserable? Happiness is fleeting, and joy dies like the cut flowers that promise it in a vase on the kitchen table.

Our focus on prosperity for ourselves means we do not spend enough time and energy returning good to the system, just on what we can get. As an employee, that encourages us to cut corners and chase get rich quick schemes. As consumers, we grow jaded about our prosperity and the physical goods it brings us.

The reality is, none of these mental tricks will take us where we really wish to go; we know that it is often the difficult times in life that people cherish the most, and grow the most from. Comfort and momentary emotions can actually be at least besides the point. And even these agents are denied to those in chronic pain, disease, or crushing poverty.

On the one hand, I agree with Professor Jordan Peterson; suffering is real and present and widespread in the world. We must indeed, with lobster-like dignity, suffer the slings and arrows of existence (and often our neighbors). There is pain and disease and old age and not being Mick Jagger to discourage us in our daily existence. There really is much to suffer, and doing so is hard.

I myself often lack the golden personality describe here as necessary for success in the world. I have been known to be considerably negative, even bitter at times. I am rather limited in my friendliness, despite my best efforts. Crap, I have often been downright rude. Being a sour type of fellow, I can use my wit to cut you verbally three ways to Sunday should you try to bloviate in my direction.

Nevertheless, I wish to describe to you one truly magical elixir that can undo all that damage in a single blow, giving us all the opportunity for improvement in both surrounding and outlook. This one true super power, that all but the most physically and mentally limited have, could turn our world upside down should we decide to make adequate use of it.

What is this magical, all powerful skill that is available to us all? It is the most simple and ignored ability in the whole world:

Doing Good.

That's it, and all of it in the whole. Now that you have

dried your eyes from the tears of laughter, indulge me as I spend the rest of this book attempting to convince you of this one thing; there is no single human activity more important than doing good. Our religions are built around it. Our laws are designed to discourage us from straying from it. Our entire societies are structured to encourage it. Still, we underestimate it's power by a million-fold, and if we were ever truly to unleash a small amount of it's potential, I believe doing good could rescue us completely from our current dreary destiny. The clouds could part and the sun could yet shine on our faces but for a little commitment to doing good.

I will not spend my time making empty promises and shallow proclamations. The difference is simple; unlike believing really hard, doing good requires work. Hard, difficult work, and lots of if. And people are unlike to give you compensation in return for it, unless we really change our ways. No, you will do what I do, sacrificing you free time to pursue things you find as valuable, and when you are done you will still buy your own damn cookie. Trust me on that one.

And yet, if we could only turn this one power into a habit, be drawn to it like a moth to a flame, we might even at this late hour change all this darkness to our own triumph. Or we may die trying, and triumph anyway. Your choice.

Doing good is critical for every civilization. Western civilization has prospered and dominated not by being cruel and violent - although through time it has been a far more than it needed to - but by learning to build a "wall of good" that competing interests have been unable to match much less tear any measurable part of it down. That wall of good is made of thousands of different pieces, from our technology to our rights to the peace that is kept in society to volunteers at the local hospital.

Today, our wall of good is under attack. There are many voices in society that have brought us a twisted message that we have done no good at all, that every bit of human progress has been built on the backs of the oppressed. That the wall of good we all rely on only exists due to racism and patriarchy and other nonsense.

This is not true, of course. The vast majority of humans who shaped the world we live in now, even people like Napoleon, believed they were doing so for the good of at least their own people. It took thousands and thousands of years of human history before we even began to comprehend the idea of peace instead of military competition, and even after that we killed more people in the name of the state during the 20th century than had been killed in all the wars previously fought.

The recent genocides in Serbia and Rwanda ought to remind us our murderous side is hidden by civil behavior, not tamed by it. It still bubbles up through the electronic halls of the internet in chat rooms and comment sections and twitter mobs. We have not given up our personal prejudices; we have picked sides that we may gang up on and verbally abuse others.

I say it is about time we commit to something more constructive than electronic abuse and psychosis-based politics. I would like to challenge you to do one good thing a week for someone else. You can think of it as pay it forward if you wish, I am not concerned. I only know that we must begin to do good, both great and small if we wish to face the resurrection of the Islamic supremacists that one day soon will attempt again to conquer Europe.

For one thing, we need to practice making sacrifice, for

sacrifice will surely be required. It costs tremendous amounts of effort and resources to beat back a committed and wily foe. For all the medieval air we get from the habits and customs of militant Islam, they also know how to live in the current times.

And I do not wish to see future generations have to suffer through the aimlessness and narcissism that has plagued us in the Westernized nations of the world. If we would permanently adopt the philosophy of doing real good in the real world to real people as our highest value I believe we could live out the idea of the Boy Scouts that has helped shape so many young men over the last century.

It certainly beats the self-serving and self-defeating philosophy of postmodernism, which is just the philosophy of suicide on a grand, slow scale. Surely we can do better in our sleep than that. (And yes, I will call you Shirley if I wish. It's my book. Write your own.)

I believe if we are wise, and we have no excuse not being wiser than those who came before us, though we're not, we could arrange our culture and society to the idea of doing good as a permanent philosophy that would round out the Boy Scout idea into a full-scale social ideal that would provide a framework for the future, so that we never need fall into the rabbit hole of dark philosophy ever again.

Life is rough, and hard, and often unfair, but doing good allows us to level the playing field at least a little. It also allows us not to succumb to negative circumstances in our lives, but gives us a tool to strike back at life's cruelty and maintain a little garden in the soul that no disaster or suffering can squelch. Even in the concentration camps of Germany there were those who planted flowers, and in doing so planted hope.

And they were rewarded for their efforts, even if a particular individual did not survive; others did, and they were able to go on, and marry and have children, and continue as unknown testimonies to the power of hope. We too can cling to silly idea that has helped so many suffer unspeakably in the past. Like it or not, we actually live in a world where ever flower matters, and every gardener really tends our souls.

So then let's all become gardeners in our own way. And this is something nearly everyone can do; even those in a wheel chair can use a mechanical grabber to pick up the trash outside their home, and the neighbors too. I do not want to see this become a competition, I just want to see us all do a little to help ourselves and our neighbors and then our civilization to be strengthened and brought together around an ideal we can all support.

We just need to do this and rejoice that we did. We need a philosophy that requires us to do good for others in return for our rights and comforts. That as a good citizen or as a good human we have a responsibility to our fellow beings to do good. Doing good in a meaningful way will have certain properties so we can be able to manage and direct our new philosophy.

1. Doing good must be universal and personal.

There are two basic types of good I care about; personal and universal. In both cases, the goal is only to do good. This is important, because this type of doing good does not involve choosing sides. You must do general good for all, regardless of who they are. The first sin of postmodernism is choosing sides. They claim they embrace the oppressed over the oppressor, but this leaves us a huge problem, determining just who is oppressed?

Is this determined through historical reference as is it for blacks in America? How does that relate to their being oppressed today? Or do we use social measurements, such as is done for the gay alphabet community? Or is it an economic and hierarchal problem as the imaginary patriarchy is? Or is it all of these things based on which description allows the strongest claims, regardless of whether there is any reality in them at all?

Doing universal good is much better, as it is not important whether or not the person receiving the good deserves it. There is no wasted energy dividing people onto artificial boxes by group or class or color. And because there is no artificial division there is no political space being used to manipulate and control others.

True compassion by definition excludes the ability to choose one over another. Our laws forbid excluding based on race or sex or religion, because real good does not arbitrarily divide. To exclude someone, it is required that they be doing real physical or economic harm to others. To do real good, the actions must do good for anyone available who is not rightly excluded, whether gay or black or Christian or Filipino or anything else in particular.

The legal assault on Masterpiece Cake Shop should never have taken place, as simply deciding not to make certain types of cakes damages no one financially or physically. Nearly every grocery in America sells boxes of cake mix, and no one will stop you from baking a cake and putting whatever message you want on it. Charlie Craig and David Mullins had every bit as much responsibility to do what was right as Mr. Phillips does. Knowing Mr. Phillips, the couple should have gone to another baker (the one that made them a cake in fact) and never bothered the ownership of Masterpiece, who never interfered with the men getting a cake somewhere else.

The reason for this refutation of exclusion is because we need as many people to participate in doing good as possible. When I donate money to homeless shelters or food banks or orphanages, I get to choose where I do good. It is better for me to be a willing participant giving what I can to something that creates good rather than useless lawyers and judges.

Is it possible to bully people and push people around? Of course it is, but then you undercut that person's reciprocal bond back to the community and others. The last thing we can afford is more disconnection, the work of the postmodernists have created far too much disconnection between people and groups in America as it is now.

2.   Doing good must be based on the best information available.

The ultimate good we can do in the West is to preserve our civilization. So we need to understand where our real failures are at and focus on fixing them. That means our work must be based on real information that we know, that we can see and be sure is correct. We do have immediate needs, socially and personally.

Is global warming one of them? Who knows? Can we point to any measureable increase in difficulty to our civilization? As technology advances and we naturally conserve more energy and use less resources will some of these more ethereal issues fix themselves? We'll have to wait and see.

On the other hand, everyone can see the issues facing Europe and Africa as Muslim territory slowly expands. The Balkans, Nigeria, and the Horn of Africa area are serious indicators that Muslims are becoming aggressive and expansionary again. It appears this expansion has broad popular support in Islamic society and certainly among the most religious.

So we focus on what we know, and keep an eye on global warming as a potential issue that may or may not materialize. And we put on our skeptic faces when we hear the hyperbole and emotional fatalistic proclamations of the Hard Left. We live in a real world, and we need to do real things to get the real effects we need.

We need to adopt a policy of "passing" those who are trying to do good and engage society according to their generally acceptable worldview. If you are inclined to reject this idea then the idea of doing any real good in the world is probably not for you. Good is done by a lot of different people in a big tent kind of way, and it has to be able to include people with a lot of different outlooks and worldviews as long as they do not arbitrarily reject people themselves without adequate reason for doing so.

We need to live in a world in which we make as much space for doing good as possible, even when it is not perfect or up to our standards. As a person of faith, I have to be willing to accept those non-believers who do good and encourage them. I recognize it is more important to keep the wagon moving in the right direction and not so much who is pushing or pulling it. So we can cooperate if we will occasionally put down the sword.

We must also recognize we live in our civilization the way corals live in their shells. Our civilizations give us structure and direction and if they are good, they allow us to build our own little part onto the basic structure. In return, our part should help to strengthen and expand the structure to which we attach ourselves. We should also through deliberative bodies be able to make some structural change to our nation as citizens and not subjects.

This is an important distinction, because the Hard Left sees the member of a nation as a subject, not a citizen. They are comfortable with the idea of the state having ultimate power, because they believe we are possessions of our government and have no rightful claim to personal space in the pubic square. Unless you are one of them, of course. We are seen as indentured servants compelled to obey the state in return for the benefits we receive.

This is destroying Westernized nations, and as society unravels, individuals members are discredited and slandered, and traditional values are scorned and destroyed. The result has been a sudden collapse of the will of basically all advanced nations as the poison of postmodernism works it way into the minds of the people, convincing them there is no hope for the future.

3. Real good must be measureable.

If we are going to start building a different focus for existence and citizenship, then we need measurable results. The incredible drop in worldwide poverty should be celebrated and widely disseminated to the public. Everyone should be made aware of the results, as they provide encouragement and satisfaction to the public for efforts well dine. To know the state of the world can provide a counterbalance to the critics and chicken littles of the world for whom the sky is always falling.

Colleges teach all kinds of mindless blather these days, and we need to counteract their focus on imaginary issues and enemies. It is apparent that we are going to need to practice living in the real world, especially younger citizens that have been to college. Our educational system no longer focuses on usable skills for their students. College seems to mostly teach people to be angry and paranoid more than anything else.

So we have to figure out how to pass on what we received from our parents and grandparents to the next generation in as best condition as possible. We need to reconnect ourselves to the values of our history. Those values did not lay the foundation for the civilization we have now because they were wrong. And we need to make sure the next generation is trained to do the same as adults themselves. One of the major errors of the Hard Left is they are believe economies are self generating, and the problem is to figure out how to extract money for everyone from them. It never occurs to them that we have to give adequate service to our communities and employers in return.

This means we need to look at the truth of the condition of the world today. I suggest the Human Progress web site as an excellent resource to begin your deprogramming. That is the first step into getting back to a healthy and productive society, each of us need to deprogram ourselves from the lies of the left. Once deprogrammed, we can then begin to renegotiate the social patterns of our nation, beginning with our families.

That also means we must make a next generation, as a part of a healthy population of adults, capable of learning to compromise and coordinate with our familial partners in mutually satisfying ways, and where not possible at least in a way that does not totally isolate the other person. Men and women are in very real ways different, and we need to figure out a middle ground publicly, socially, culturally, and personally in order to come to a way in which we hold one another to important values while allowing as much freedom as possible.

We need to require that students in high school need to learn the basics of finance, personal relationships, and philosophy. Colleges should be required to have students take classes to reinforce these understandings. If Western universities do not at least prepare students to be useful citizens then all their research is in vain.

As it stands, Muslim civilization is growing while the Westernized world is beginning to shrink rapidly. If we do not care about others, this is fine. But we have to see our individual nations as a set of bulwarks that need bracing with population growth of loyal citizens to meet that of our competitor. But if we leave the world to the Muslim civilization then all Western ideals will be destroyed and may never be resurrected at all.

The idea that Muslim civilization will moderate is the worst kind of fantabulism possible. I was born in 1963, 55 years ago. Of all those nations which were majority Muslim at that time, you can not name a single one that has become more moderate in both society and governance. And in another 55 years, the population balance will be well into the shift to Muslim domination. If may be so far along at that point in fact that military conflict may be unavoidable if we have not already matched the population growth of Islam by then.

Even if in another 500 years the natural social growth of Islam would be to moderation, it will not happen if centuries before then Islam does come to dominate the world. Once in control it will have overseen a couple of hundred years or more of an unchallenged new dark age.

This would be disastrous, as without any competition from an alternate civilization any impulse to moderation will be easily squelched.

We must get our act together to decide ways we can live together in peace as adults willing to make the sacrifices necessary to give us and our civilization a fighting chance to hold its own in the long run – the ultimate earthly good.

We have a lot of doing good to get to, and the future of mankind depends on our success. What we will face over the next 30 years will pull us back to reality or it will not. One way leaves the world in darkness and the other may not.

We'll decide.

ONE:
GOOD BY ANY OTHER NAME

Self-evident. That is the term the founders of the United States used to describe the position of the individual and their claim to rights of action in the world. Life, liberty, and the pursuit of happiness. It seems so simple, but for those who live in the U.S. it has become a tangled ball of wiring that is difficult to follow in one sweep. Like the wires in your entertainment system.

It is so hard to disentangle these conflicting ideas about such a simple proposition. Societies and individuals have their own views on the importance of these three terms. We are ambivalent much of the time that they mean anything, and mostly vocal from the place of our own desires. Thus, the very first thing we have to look at, even at the individual level is that people (mostly) want to be happy.

It's true, at least usually. There is something about humans that we are geared towards happiness. There are a few people in every society that are not happy and who do not want to be, but they are fairly few and far between. Still, they exist, and because they are often volatile we need pay them attention. For the rest of us, we have such a strong bent towards happiness that advertisers will spend billions of dollars explaining why we would be so much happier if we just used the right toothpaste. Face it, we all like happy. We just don't know how to make it last.

This is difficult on it's own, because happiness is it's own can of worms that crawl off in a million different directions in a society. Two gay men who are married want to pursue happiness. So does the Christian living down the street. So does the crack dealer and serial killer. Life, liberty and the pursuit of happiness gets messy really fast. And somehow, if we wish to live in a peaceful society we have take the time and effort to sort this all out. For the rest of our sakes we might need make the serial killer unhappy. (Ok, cereal killer for all you Al Gore fans. But just this once. I'm super cereal about it.)

Of course everyone does not want to be happy. Every society has a small number of psychopaths and mentally unstable people who do not want to be happy. They torture animals and grow up to be those serial killers and in doing so add nothing of value to our philosophical conversation. So we can set them aside, and simply stick with nearly everyone wants to be happy.

However, the pursuit of happiness is not guaranteed. Plenty of people do not really get there. And many that do, only do so partly. They get to have the family they want but they have a nasty job cleaning port-a-potties or driving a trash truck for a living. Other people do not get there due to physical disability or mental disability. We all have our limitations, and the path to adulthood is the acceptance of our weaknesses as well as our strenths.

We lie to our kids and tell them they can do whatever they want to in life. It's a horrible practice that is more damaging than anything else. A kid in a wheelchair will never be an NBA star. Someone who is bad in math will suck as an accountant, and should probably do something else for a living (or expect to be pretty poor).

Our problem is we want to believe. We see happiness as a right - ergo the reason the baker is sued by the gay couple in the first place. They take the worst possible view of happiness; that other people are responsible for making them happy. You'll never get there that way. We need to shake this silly and harmful idea off. Happiness is the result of a lot of other actions. Yes, people like Bill Gates and Elon Musk are presently rich and at least modestly happy. But it took them a lot of time and an incredible amount of struggle and work to get there, and without that work and struggle they would neither be as rich nor as happy as they are. And even now they struggle, as we all who are living do.

Happiness is a product you produce through your attitude and actions. And you have to do a lot of work to get a little happiness back. It's kind of like gathering maple sap for syrup. A lot of effort gets you a little sweetness. This leaves each of us with the question of how much happiness do we want, and how hard are we willing to work for it?

For most, 40 hours a week is it. It buys you minimal happiness as long as nothing particularly bad happens. Things that upset everyday life can rob such a person of all or nearly all of the happiness they managed to scrape together with their minimal efforts. Most people live on this street.

Almost all of the remaining people want more

happiness than that, and they work a little harder at it, both at home and at work. They have some less free time for golfing and crack use, but they are more interested in work-life balance as many of them wish to both provide for their children and spend time with the family.

A thin sliver are willing to work the way Bill Gates and Elon Musk do. They worry about gaining and doing things and are internally driven to be less worried about others. Some of them have excellent relations with their wives in particular if they really do retire the way Bill Gates has. The others have varying levels of happiness in family life and with others. It depends on the personality of the person. They also tend to be the ones who push the borders of technology and business and provide the products we all enjoy so much.

So we can't agree on what kind and how much happiness we want, and how much effort we are willing to put into pursuing it (and that motivation may vary over a lifetime). What can we then agree on? Is there something around which we can agree that allows us to pursue our own happiness and let others pursue their happiness as well?

I believe there is, but I think looking at happiness as a right and our grasping for it and the process of making happiness is looking in the wrong direction. These things are far too specific, and they do not allow us in general to see our actions in a way that gives us space when we deal with others. We need to look at a more generic base principle that gives us identity separate from others and is fit for everyday use.

Trust me, I am well aware the meaning of life has been struggled with by philosophers throughout the centuries. I am aware that we have been provided quite a few crazy answers that somehow are supposed to solve all our problems. Nietzsche thought everything would magically be better somehow if we all thought God was dead – why, no one seems to know.

Postmodernism gives us even less to live for. So what if all of human activity is a struggle for power? That's no proof you should weld it, or would actually do so for the right reasons. And it is certainly no proof you would do the right thing with it should you gain power. You might even be right in a particular area about what a specific problem is and still not have a good solution (hint; you don't if you are on the Hard Left).

None of those things are enough to give us meaning or direction, because they lack use and connection as based on individual characteristics. I think we need to look at the type of doable, functional type of meaning for our lives and existence that will do us much more good than trying to make it mystical or some grand scheme to fix history which can never be changed. Yet, as we look at this principle of doing good, we will see it does exactly that. Here is my suggestion:

All of these tools we have as human beings have given us great powers beyond of those of other animals. But there is one specific use that all of these tools tend to lend themselves to; Doing Good. More than anything else the meaning of life is to do good. We are beings designed (or created for those of us who prefer) to do good.

This is the one singular power we have that no other species has. Not a singer flower blooms in order to make a field beautiful. Not a single butterfly flits from flower to flower because the poor plants need to be pollinated. Trees do not try to grow a little taller because the children playing in the yard below could use the shade and protection from the elements.

Let me give you how rare and how limited to humans this ability really is; on extremely rare occasions that often show up on the internet a handful of times a year, animals do this with the young of other species, but it tends to be instinctive even then. Like the cat that adopts a young pup that lost it's mother, or the young fox and doe playing together because even as an adult fox deer are to large and fast for foxes to hunt anyway.

As for the lions taking down an antelope, they are not doing any favors to their prey at all. Only humans intentionally raise leopard cubs or open food kitchens or create the technology that makes our lives better. And even in the case of Apple, they as a business do indeed exist to make money, but no one pays for stuff regularly that makes their lives worse. Even businesses must provide good intrinsically in their products or they will go out of business.

Doing good then is intrinsic in the DNA of every society on earth. We measure every product and service by its measure. And every individual and every movement has ideas of what types of good they want and will make them happy. Government happens when those ideas of personal and group good come into conflict. But there can be no doubt that society revolves around a series of ideas what good is.

The ability to do and demand good makes us nearly godlike in our power. People don't generally fight over food in the streets, at least in the first world, and we do not worry about a raiding party of grunting people with clubs from the next business marching over and raiding our office and dragging our secretary away. Even the largest schools of fish can cooperate on only a primitive level compared to the smallest rural Sheriff's Department.

So let me put this into a more specific point; despite all the good done by all the people in the world, only you can do good with and in your own life. Do yourself a favor, and put this book down and go think on that for a while, because your doing good can be critical when you are hiding a family while you're living in a police state. We think we have a rugged civilization that was destined to rule through our superiority, but in truth over the passing times our history civilization has often hung by a thread.

It is vital that more good than evil be done in the world. Society breaks down when evil reigns. We can lose our humanity when we allow destructive ideas teach us to hate. That makes it vital that you do good. Like a row of dominoes, one thing trips another until destruction becomes a given. So doing good keeps the wolf from our own door. And with this power we have a wonderful gift; we cannot know the future, so cannot tell what good act will lead to the next important influence ahead of time. We would not know of Anne Frank if she had not been hidden long enough to keep her diary.

This leaves it up to us to look at the world and decide where we can use our resources to do the most good. It is a hit and miss endeavor, true enough, but doing good regularly returns a level of results to us and the world around us far beyond what pursuing happiness could ever do. And widespread levels of good grease the wheels of the pursuit of happiness. No one from the government is going to break into your house and take anything you own, outside of harmful materials such as child porn, and burn your possessions for political reasons in America. Yes, there are thieves and burglars and somewhere around 15 neo-Nazis, but most homes will never be broken into or damaged. That means any stuff you accumulate to help make you happy is relatively secure for you to keep as long as you want.

Same thing with activities. Police do not raid the local Fred Astaire studio because all that sensual dancing is corrupting society. We are not even all that hard on drug addicts and axe murderers, because American society is willing to allow a small amount of disorder as simply affordable in order to allow more good. But not too much.

If I have not convinced you, that is fine. But I believe is self-evident that Doing Good is the central meaning for human existence. The attitude of pitching in to society is as important as the acts themselves and the motivation it can give you to act. It is a special power that is a part of the hidden divinity of our existence. Doing good is the most valuable thing you can do.

But that doesn't make it easy.

TWO:
LIFE IS A MESS

What a train wreck. What a disaster. Look around at the world. Floods. Hurricanes. Volcanoes. The old maxim seems true; everything that can go wrong....is going wrong. And it's not just mother nature either. It's everything. Most of us feel financially like we are barely hanging on to the edge of a cliff at the Grand Canyon. And that is here in America. I do not know what hope people in Africa hang onto.

How do we deal with it all? Babies born with heart defects. Yellow fever and malaria. Think about that—the most dangerous creature in the world is a little insect called the mosquito. The Dodo bird is extinct, but we have absolutely no power to get rid of a little insect that is more deadly than any carnivore.

Suffering. It takes all our happiness and squishes it like a bug. Disease, age, war, natural disasters all take our happiness and smushes it in the great gears of misery that grind on unstoppable. There are lots of sources to blame.

The media, the government, the wicked boss, there are lots of people to point fingers at. We even blame God. The buck actually stops there, right?

It's downright depressing I say. Civilization has hung by a thread since day one. Don't believe me? Imagine what it would be like here just in America if we had another Dust Bowl type drought. Hitler came within a hair's breath of winning the summer he invaded France, and again the next summer when he invaded Russia. The Russians had the U.S. on the run during the 1970's or so it seemed at the time. Only the victory over the Muslims at Battle of Tours made our civilization possible to start with. Likewise the Battle of Vienna against the Turks a few centuries later. Only the arrival of American troops saved the French at Bellamy Wood. Lee had three chances to win the Battle of Gettysburg, one each day.

I could go on and on with my little list. By the most slender of threads civilization has come through dozens of times. Verdun. Kursk. El Alamein. Waterloo. Often it was literally an individual that saved civilization. Churchill. Halsey. Nelson. Civil society itself has been guided and built by men named Lincoln, King, and Kennedy. Even bringing us to the future, to drop our prejudices, has been a monumental task. We've often hung in the balance to the last man.

Yet despite the evidence we stubbornly refuse to allow for the truth of human nature. We reject the truth that both light and dark live in the human heart in like measure. The Hard Left constantly portrays their enemies as having only the worst of intentions, yet deny that the whole of the human race teeters on the edge of darkness. Humans will fight tooth and nail to deny that they could ever be wrong much less evil. That we might look at the contents of our own hearts is beyond reason to ask. So we fight to maintain our vanity, that our ego may not be strained.

We lie about civilization itself, and our place in it. We speak of ourselves as having "evolved" as if we are but a little training better than the barbarians we come from. We deny that civilized behavior is a learned set of habits, preferring to believe that our instinct is to goodness when it clearly is not. We will hear not the hard truth that only our disposition to social behavior is natural, and the actual learning of civilized behavior is done through hard, disciplined effort to teach and much practice in learning.

So much of what we need is merely a matter of humility, a deadly poison to the modern ego. We prefer "tolerance" that our own sensitivities might one day be ignored in return. And in all of it, we do not consider the chains we place on our own souls. Then we strangely enough find ourselves in an imperfect world wracked with violence and loneliness for which we need a scapegoat.

Politically, we are at each other's throats right now. The western world has begun to spiral out of control, and there is a certain segment of our population that seems to be rooting for our destruction. A real emergency might push us over the edge. Throw in some serious hunger and see how bad it gets. Yet here we are, with computers and spaceships and GMO food that increases crop yields and feeds the world.

These things are not all the same of course. They are different areas of human activity, but they are also areas in which humans have struggled for centuries. War and disaster and pestilence has been our lot for millennia. Yet I wish you to notice a certain pattern that appears when it comes to struggle and suffering: Doing Good is amplified in the midst of struggle and pain.

An honest assessment shows doing good has been an incredible success; the world has improved vastly over the last couple of centuries. Marx thought that capitalism would make the workers poorer, but the average British citizen grew three times richer during the 65 years of his life according to Prager U. Slowly over time, the lot of most of the world has improved since the time of Christ. Living in Arizona, I get to see the crude structures the Native Americans lived in when the Spanish arrived a few centuries ago. The cheapest mobile home is a palace in comparison.

So despite the naysayers and the scrooges of the world, doing good is the one powerful force of the human race that is rarely without benefit. We can grease the skids toward a positive future with it. We can uphold our real core values and turn back those who wish to polarize and destroy. We too can hold this thread in our hands and refuse to let it break.

But this requires commitment above all. We must as a whole society be utterly committed to doing good, to seeing ourselves as part of a team – even on the same team. We have to become our own Power Rangers for good. We don't need corny outfits or bad karate moves, we need a commitment to ourselves and each other that if we manage to do enough good, we might save the world.

Our mindset, that volunteering is largely for rich people and students prepping for college and retirees needs to change. Doing something, anything at all, must become a universal responsibility. We all should be held to doing something, even if just a little. But it needs to be a cultural understanding and a social norm rather than a legal requirement.

Commitment to doing what good we can is not so

difficult.　　But we need to be intentional, everyday, unwaveringly committed to the good of our families, communities, and civilization.　This is only going to work if we are willing to get enough through the system to turn the ship.　A civilization is large, and slow to change in good ways, yet takes on water so easily.　Postmodernists seek to maximize the leaks as self-destruction is the only good for them.

We who wish to prosper in our clearly superior civilization need to treat this like a marathon.　Every generation build the layer on which the next one starts. We must invest and look forward, and make plans and keep to them.　We need to be self disciplined so that we do not waver, as it will take a lot of effort to get our of our doldrums and turn things around.

But it is worth it, just as it always has been throughout the centuries.　We are locked in this guided cage called the world, and we have no other real way to contribute to reality.　It is incredibly important to understand and maintain the realization that reality is far more valuable than our personal worlds, whether digital or imaginary-not that there is any real difference.

Make the commitment today.

THREE:
NOT A HERO

We are not the hero, at least not here, today. We pursue only our own interests, betraying those ideals we say are important. We also know this. Betrayal is a disease as common as herpes, only the outbreaks are far more universal. Become a notorious traitor, and you too may become famous. Your name can drip off the lips just as Quisling and Benedict Arnold. Yet betrayal is a game we play as nearly as much as our video games.

We're not the heroes - not now. Not here. Not doing the crappy, mindless stuff we do that we use to take our minds off the stuff we need to be working through. Modern society right down to the individual can be stereotyped by a single word: avoidance.

And brother, we are experts. We avoid it all. Our families, our neighbors, our lovers and friends, and above all, ourselves. Nope, we're not the Champions. We're an ocean away. A billion dollars short.

It might not be so bad if we could just paddle in the right direction at least, but we can't even do that with consistency. Worse than anything, we have the frustrating capacity to make ourselves mentally ill. We do it all the time. The Nazis were the symptom of a people who were out of their minds, quite literally. So mentally ill they were willing to work as guards in concentration camps and feed Jews to the ovens.

We are ridiculously naïve. We believe any shyster who comes along. Look at all the used car lots in any major American city. They make their money off you. We take deadly poisons just 'cause our doctor says to; ever hear of diethylstilbestrol (DES)? Your grandma did, and millions took it. That explains some of the crazy:

https://www.reuters.com/article/us-health-adhd-des/banned-pregnancy-drug-tied-to-adhd-generations-later-idUSKCN1IN2OW

But the Nazi's were far from the only crazies on the block; the Soviet Union, the Cultural Revolution of China, the Khmer Rouge, the Rwandan genocide, all the same self-made crazy town. It's in us just like a virus, springing up in new and unexpected places, like in the minds of the American Left. In the United States, just as in much of the West, College doesn't teach you the truth about life or give you marketable skills, it teaches you how to be mentally ill. It gives you the tools, the training and the programming necessary to be a danger to yourself and others.

We lie and want to see the good in others, but that is not a realistic view of the world. A good chunk of humanity have darker motivations, and resist the good they see in the world. They are ideologues, or seek revenge or simply are inflexible about their own cultural habits and beliefs.

Make no mistake about it, the 100-million plus dead from the last century are more than from all the wars and strife before it combined. And every single drop was shed for no reason other than the human capacity for self-induced psychosis. Worse, we have obviously not learned the tiniest thing from the slaughter, as it is apparent there is a good-sized plurality if not majority that seems dandy for round two.

The problem is the next time won't be so exciting and romantic. The next time, if we're lucky, a few survivors will be crawling out of the rubble lost and hurting and radioactive and needing to start civilization over again. Even that will not be enough I fear.

I don't know if there is an answer to our predicament, either. We have this craving for drama, for having an enemy, for having someone to build our bulwarks against. Or we waffle, holding out the greyed flowers of appeasement because we fear the looming confrontation. We are much as Churchill stereotyped us; always doing the right thing, after we have tried everything else.

There may not be a cure, but there may be enough of an antidote, should we choose it, to allow us to continue forward. Here again, I must be the bearer of bad news; I think it incredibly unlikely we are going to be willing to take our medicine, as mild as it may be. The only hope we have is to change the story, to make the decision to take up the banner of good (great is for business leaders).

We need to teach ourselves that doing good is the highest ideal we can reach, that doing good is what makes us great, as this book is my attempt at. Doing good has to be the brass ring we reach for as individuals and as a society.   There is one caveat; we have to give up the distorted ideas of social good propagated by the Hard Left. Paranoia is not the basis for a workable society.

That means the gay men who went to Masterpiece Cake Shop should be shamed for not doing good, as they are individually responsible to do good to others just as much as anyone else. If you make plans to oppress and harm another, you are not doing good and deserve to suffer the consequences.

That means we take a really balanced assessment of ourselves and our history. We live in a bizarre world in which those on the left say they believe that people are basically good, yet deny that anyone in power in an advanced society has ever done good and we do not do so now. Those who are conservative tend to believe that all humans are at least vulnerable to corruption, yet insist on denying the history of those they base their ethics on, regardless of how low they were in real life.

Here in the real world, Thomas Jefferson was a slave owner and a bit of a creep with it. On the other hand, he helped put into motion a process that would eventually tear down the very slavery he was involved in. That has always been the way this works, and it always will be. The modern leftist believes they are superior than those who came before them, even though the morals they purport to carry came from those flawed forebears just like everything else we have has been handed down over time. And there is certainly no indication their personal morals aren't the worst in human history.

It is shocking to me to watch mere mortals puff on about how superior they are. They do not realize they have merely replaced the racial superiority of the Germans with the ethical superiority of the communists.   But perfection is imaginary. None of us are perfect, those demanding perfection the least perfect of all as they cannot see their demand is beyond their grasp.

Everything is always being upgraded, improved, negotiated in the real world. Life moves forward in steps, not Great Leaps. Everything, even technology, slogs along at it's own pace. We will get where we are going not through bulldozing civilization over and starting anew but by fixing up our part of it, which every human being has a responsibility to do.

We have a responsibility to remain engaged, to not check out and play video games all day. We are responsible for what our children inherit, and the mark we leave on history. We are responsible for how we treat our enemies, our friends our fellow citizens and those who cannot do for themselves. We are responsible for teaching the next generation truth and actual right from wrong rather than the postmodernist pabulum our children are fed at school.

Existence carries a heavy price tag that none of us ever asked for. Yet here we are, and we **can** do those things that are required of us. That which is necessary may not be fun, but that does not lessen the urgency of our charge. We must do good anyway, and take our responsibility honestly and earnestly.

There is no other way to exist. Or at least not one that matters.

FOUR:
THE LAST BOY SCOUT

We've been here before, you know. According to King Solomon, there is nothing new under the sun, and at least where it comes to human psychosis this seems reasonably true. We are not the first generation of people to lose our footing due to technological progress.

If you would like a full overview, I would direct you to The Art of Manliness web page. It is a fascinating read:

https://www.artofmanliness.com/articles/call-new-strenuous-age/?fbclid=IwAR3V7gSDoEvDXK-wgA9tBtK3IaRTz7ApdqxIVIPw4bC_FfwQiRgvxxRTMJA

It appears to me the description given by the Art of Manliness web site pretty much accurately describes how society gets disrupted by technology and social change. I do believe the ease created by the increased amount of free time can be a negative power to those who are not disciplined enough to channel their energies on their own.

Mechanical malfunction of the mind is a physical defect, but it is possible to short-circuit your own mind if you are given the time and encouragement.

The vast majority of people struggle with boredom, and I think there is a psychological pathway in our minds that sees inactivity as a negative. I am not sure that someone sitting in their living room day after day because they are unemployed is not going through the same mental process someone in prison goes through siting in their cell day after day. The result is a sense of general malaise and discontentment.

Postmodernism adds an incredible punch to this by describing the world as a total wreck, and prescribes an antidote no one in their right mind wants to live through. When people are told they need to die because they are white or male or heterosexual something is deeply wrong with society. Worse, when this seems totally unfixable, it can take what little wind there is right out of your sails. In a lot of ways, we really are adrift in an ocean of indifference. We are told by those who we entrust to educate us that we are worthless and useless, and all we can do is make life worse with our best efforts. Depression is a natural response.

The good news is, the last time we were here, we did overcome our malaise. And we did it by learning to challenge ourselves, and restore a sense of manhood. We brought ourselves out of our funk by mastering things around us and creating competence in ourselves. It worked like a charm, and just in time, too; only a few years later the guns of August would announce the First World War, followed by a second one even more terrible and bloody.

Our last recovery was helped by the expansion of

parks, clubs, and ministries that catered to the new sense of virility in society. Both the YMCA and the Boy Scouts were created as a result of the enthusiasm that the renewal of our culture brought. It got us through a lot, from the Great Depression to putting a man on the moon. But calls for a new Strenuous Age will do us no good under the current circumstances.

The main reason is postmodernism itself. As the first ideal of the movement is that all human endeavor is a struggle between the powerful and the powerless, those on the wrong list cannot positively take part in society. Being a white male basically locks you out of being able to contribute, and any efforts you may make are automatically contaminated by your whiteness and maleness.

The second reason we cannot count on the general renewal of social vigor to work through a new strenuousness of heart is simple; there is no end to serve as a motivating force and as a focus towards which to direct our efforts. If you like to hike Camelback Mountain, as I do, chances are you are already doing so, at least as far as you are motivated to get up and go. It's there, it is open to be climbed, and people do so all day long.

But that's preaching to the choir, as the old saying goes. That will not impel converts, or those converts to begin working towards self-improvement much less make a habit out of their competence. What we need is a reason to get our of bed every morning. What we need is a reason to turn off the console and put the controller down and go do these other things. We need a reason for asking others to re-engage in a life that has handed out some hard lumps lately.

We need a goal in mind, one general enough to allow anyone who desires to participate and specific enough to have meaning. The practice of doing good fits the bill perfectly. Why should you get off the couch and get some exercise? Because life is unpredictable, so in an emergency you might find yourself in a boat rescuing your neighbors.

Because you might find your self with other likeminded people in the middle of a riot, and you need to be prepared to defend yourself and your family. Because you might end up joining some of your neighbors to put up new playground equipment in your neighborhood park. Because you can make a child a bed with a little plywood and some hand tools if you know how.

Because there is a lot of work to be done in the world feeding the hungry and sheltering the homeless, and you need to start doing your part. Here's the deal; no one can deny the good you can do. What happens is your accuser is exposed as the puppet they are when they try to discredit those who are doing good. Many criticize Mother Theresa, yet she is still revered. Any mark you earn for doing good in society is permanent like that.

It gives lie to the charges the postmodernists make against you, that you are incapable because of the accident of your birth for doing good. In fact, doing good in the sense I am speaking of proves the very opposite of the postmodernist argument; that regular people can effect their neighbors to the positive, that power does not need to be the highest goal of the individual (or the fanciful groups they support) and that we are all actually the same as human beings and not the imaginary monsters we are too often portrayed as.

If we are to enter into a second period of social renewal, we need more than a rebellious spirit to do so. We need a goal, an aim. Something to shoot for that makes the effort worthwhile every day. If we renew ourselves around the idea we are gong to be made vessels to carry good into the world we might yet strike the match that sets the entire book aflame.

Would it not be wonderful to push back against the postmodern propaganda with more than mumbled confessions and shame? Would it not be much better to be able to answer, "I volunteered at ____ yesterday. What did you do that was useful?"

I do agree with the Art of Manliness site that we do need a new Strenuous Age. But we need more than a modern version of camping in the woods. We need to make a movement that will impact society and relieve those in need and desire our help. We need to be prepared to do good the same way those in the National Guard do; as a serious enough endeavor we keep ourselves prepared.

That preparedness is the tool that will allow us to whittle away at the chains of hyper-selfishness we have shackled ourselves with. It allows us to both claim and see that the culture we created in the West, our civilization itself can indeed function the way our wise men over the centuries have suggested we can. That we can be earnest and real, not just the hypocritical cads the Hard Left claims we all are.

Once we understand what we can be, individually, together, voluntarily, we may then open the door to communicating and acting on the serious failure to procreate. And having the real support of the community and our neighbors, we just may find ourselves willing to expand the borders of our tents with the children that are not the key to our future but are the very thing itself.

It is a long shot, but I think it is the only shot we have. If we do not turn the narrative of our society somehow, we will be under the gun by 2100, as more and more of Europe falls under the dark tide of Islam. Time is short, and we need to make allies into friends and enemies into allies if we are to survive.

We need a new social contract that goes beyond the letter of the law to the spirit of our humanity. Only then, when we all make the commitment that as we all pitch in and do good to one another can we keep the promise we will leave no one behind. And if we keep that promise we can forge new connections to those around us, and that is good for us all.

Our enemies are stronger than we think, and their power is real. We need a new Strenuous Age in order to defeat them. So be strenuous to do good, and anxious for the opportunities to do so. That is how you build a better tomorrow.

One good thing at a time.

FIVE:
HOW TO BE A SUPERHERO

You have been lied to. Literally, unequivocally, absolutely lied to. It's the biggest lie ever told in human history: Do what makes you happy. If you do what makes you happy, you will never work another day in your life.

No, you won't work another day in your life. You will lie on you bed all afternoon doodling or listening to music until your lack of income makes you homeless. What a load of fresh crap. Unless you're Justin Bieber you can forget about this. But you should try as long as what you want to do is for real connected to potential income or public good. Doodling may not count, as it depends on the art market in your area.

But it you want to be a superhero and ensure you make an impact on the world, I have the secret on what you *should* do; the thing that makes you crazy. The thing that makes you insane. That makes that vein on your forehead stick out. That makes you want to scream at people and throw office furniture. Because here's the secret to doing good: That's your calling. Do you hear me?

THAT'S YOUR CALLING.

It may pay your bills or not, but that's what you should be doing. Consider your job the thing you do to support your calling, but do the things you need to in order to fix what makes you crazy. Because chances are, that will make a lot of other people's lives better too. Twenty years ago, there was no Wounded Warrior Project. But someone decided it was not acceptable for our veterans not to get critical care when they came home so they did something about it.

At one time there was no Red Cross, no Special Olympics, no Salvation Army, no Feed the Children. All these organizations were started by people who saw a problem and could not let it be. So they did what they needed to do - they started to work, to give, to fight to do something about the problem they were confronted with.

You don't have to start a whole new organization. You can most likely find people doing what you want to do and join them. Maybe support something financially. But what you find annoying is far more important than you could ever imagine to your future. And all of those people you help, known or unknown, will still be affected by your efforts, and that makes you indeed a superhero.

In fact, I would suggest that the first thing you want to consider if you are thinking about getting married is to make sure you and your spouse have the same calling. Having the same annoyances and same attitudes will make it easier to be a team. Most marriages are really just two individuals pursuing their own interests all week, and usually on the weekends too. And even on weekends, most couples just happened to be entertained by the same things. Occasionally.

A husband and wife who are just activity partners will drag each other away from the things that they each want to do in terms of calling. This is a horrible thing for society, and it stresses a marriage already based on scant little.

I can not remember who it was now, but I heard an interview over the last few years of a successful college head coach recalling what it was like when he was a kid and his father was a college coach. He recalled how on Friday nights, his mom would make a big pot of spaghetti as the recruited kid had dinner with the family. They would let the kid being recruited basically eat all he wanted as they got to know him and talk about his decision of where to attend and play.

Now of course, head coaches make millions and highly recruited kids go on school visits like rock stars touring the country. But once upon a time, recruiting was a personal and intimate endeavor and wives were (and still are) important parts of the team. That is the sacrifice and effort it really takes to do something important in a high school kids' life and future. There are a whole lot of people who would consider the long hours and year-round schedules to be too big a sacrifice. Some people don't want to be cops or firefighters either, and that is perfectly OK. But the world would sure be a better place if every household was made up of a couple who agreed to go out in the world and work on a particular issue in their spare time one hour a week.

I know of many solid couples, but the best always have this kind of thing in common. I know one couple who were led to religious ministry. I know another couple who are both writers, on some important subjects. I have seen for myself having that connection as co-laborers about important matters have enriched their lives immeasurably and it shows. They have great relationships though they have been through some incredibly situations. Opposites may attract, but they also normally explode.

If you were to follow my good advice and make the effort necessary to help tackle the issues of the world, you might not just improve the lives of others but also of your own. That should be the best motivation you can receive. Be a superhero today and make a difference.

SIX:
HEARTS IN A JAR

So why do we find it so difficult to maintain our balance, not to be led away by the glitz and glamour of technology and entertainment? Because it is easy to passively watch. Because resisting it requires effort. And great effort can only come from one place: the human spirit, of which we have a tremendous deficit in the world. Nothing I say, no commitment we make will matter a single bit if we cannot put forth the great effort necessary to overcome. And few have even the smallest measure of it in our time.

We mistake anger for spirit most of the time. But there is a difference between someone in Russia or Greece or Iran being upset with their poor luck in location of birth and the kind of human spirit the Greeks were speaking of. Even in Sparta that spirit was twisted into forms that were cruel and not part of what it means to act from a whole heart.

What does this spirit of the human heart look like? It

looks like the Americans during and after World War 2. During the war, they demanded unconditional surrender, not stopping until they overran Germany and dropped nuclear weapons on Japan twice to compel them to surrender. After the war, it looked like the Marshall Plan, and the decision to allow the Japanese Emperor to remain on the throne.

It's not just victorious in battle, it's also self confident to rightly measure on a wider scale that allows for as much good as possible - even on recent enemies that caused death and suffering on an unprecedented scale. The real human spirit is embodied in the way those responded not just to the fighting but to the people who were conquered when the fighting was over.

I can think of only a handful of humans these days I would infer as having that kind of heart. It is desperately missing, and even more desperately needed. But heart is difficult to find once lost and history is littered with those who were unable to reconnect the dead lines of communication to theirs in an emergency. Danger and tragedy only brings out the best in us in the best in us.

That will no longer do. I want you to understand one thing very clearly; they want us dead. That's why all of a sudden there are voices speaking out and saying it. Now, the idea that "white people need to die out" is publicly expressed and supported by a plurality of the citizens of the West. Yes, Treblinka and Auschwitz are closed, but we mistook peace for victory. The truth is the gas chambers have never truly shut down, they just took other forms.

For a long time, they were partially hidden behind the high walls of the Iron Curtain and the bamboo wall of the Chinese. They were not a danger to the West, until the two rotten seeds of colonialism and postmodernism sprouted. And now all of a sudden the camps are back, but in a different form. We live in a mental gulag today, waiting our turn to die. The mental prison in which we find ourselves is just as deadly as the gas chambers in Germany ever were.

We are in prison, walled in by the accusations of oppression and historical wrongs. We have mental bars of guilt and shame over a history we have no power to change. Our prison guards are the modern companions of narcissism and depression. We are chained by the accusations of greed and selfishness and racism.

So whence comes this sudden move towards open genocide? It comes from the fact those on the Hard Left believe we robbed them. To many on the left, the Soviet Union was the worker's paradise they wanted for all the world. But they were outnumbered by the good people in the West who happened to be able to make the necessary efforts to see the Soviet Union collapse. That is why they hate us so much.

So for a growing portion of the new Hard Left, our current genocide is intentional. Western civilization and all it's supporters are traitors to them. For them, the destruction of our civilization is of prime importance, and they have worked diligently to build our mind prison through persuading us we deserve to die off. And we, not paying attention, have gone along willingly.

Every person beaten by an Antifa thug, every downtick of the native population of Japan or Germany or Sweden, every Christian in prison in China, they are all another body fed to the mental ovens in this worldwide concentration camp. Their goal is to weaken us to the point they can turn us over to the Muslims and Africans and allow them to finish the work they are too cowardly to complete themselves. It is genocide, just as surely as it was in Germany and as real as any physical place in the world. And one day, if we allow it, we will be in real cages once again.

Evil men all around the world are struggling to gain power in order to destroy those who are good, that they may avenge the death of their dreams. They are not trying to build a better world. They are not trying to make up for the errors of our past. They intend not only to destroy Western civilization, but every edifice of good governance everywhere. And not only that, but they intend to kill, through depressing fertility rates via propaganda and modern comforts, every single one of us who live for the good.

And we have gone along with it, falsely believing we had dispatched our enemies. We sacrificed our children to Moleck in return for television and a small pension when we are old. We cannot let them win like this. Collusion with the enemy is treason and is unacceptable. That should be crystal clear to you now.

So how do you start to reclaim your heart from the propaganda prison of the Hard Left? I am gong to help you get started, by telling you one simple thing:

You do not deserve to die.

Do you hear me? Really hear me? If you get nothing else at all out of these books, I need you to get this deep into your soul; You do not deserve to die. Every single civilization on the face of the planet has made both horrible acts of cruelty and wonderful contributions to the world. We do not deserve to die for this. We deserve to live.

You deserve to live. To live the best life you can. To continue to give our best to our families, our communities, and our countries. To continue to have the freedom to build the things that make the world work and our lives better.

The lies of the enemies are not our final destination and we do not have to accept their pronouncements. We do not have to live in the mental prison the postmodernists have built for us. We can be free to live and believe what we wish about the world, and no one can stop us. But we have to stand up and fight for our rights. They won't come easily. Postmodernists mean it when they explain how they see us as the root of all evil in the world. They mean it when they say they are going to snuff it - snuff *us* - out.

We must get our hearts back. We need to have more than generic emotional responses to life, but real love. We can fix all if only we will really learn to love enough to do. This is where it gets difficult, because I do not know how to teach you how to love. This you are going to have to learn on your own.

But I love a lot of things, including my Christian faith. I love the civilization I was born into. I love people from all around the world. I have a special affinity for those who I think are trying to do the right thing, like the people of Taiwan. But I don't exactly know what I mean by love other than I love them.

They say personal love comes and goes, but that is not this. My experience is that love is both an emotional attachment but also a commitment to connect to people. I don't know if that is learned. I don't know if you can learn it. I've always had it, and I can't explain it fully. It's like asking me what beauty is – I don't know, but I know what I appreciate.

So I have to leave you sort of on your own here. All I can do is say that it is vital if we are going to continue for you to have an emotional connection to the people on this planet. The good people of the world need you desperately. Hardship is insufferable if you do not have things and people you love more than your difficulties and pain.

I can only suggest that you find a way to come to recognize you are loved, that we are all loved, by God. Then it seems love comes so much easier because if you are in God's hand the rest is not so much about your comfort. Learning to appreciate all this life has given you would make a great grounding for loving others. But regardless of how you come about it, you absolutely have to find a way to open your heart to loving the people of the world we live in.

You must find a way to do it. Right now, today, there are villages in Japan that have been completely abandoned, shrines and everything, because we have not figured out to fight back and reclaim ourselves. We have already lost much in Japan alone, and we sill continue to lose until one day not long from now we will lose our very future.

The real reason those villages are empty is the same one people in America are dying from opiates. To be a human is to be a particular person, in a particular place and time, not just some creature having organized thoughts. Yes, you can make some assumptions such as Matt Dillahunty and Sam Harris does about having a moral code, but that is not the real problem.

No moral code can tell you why YOU matter. Is not

being robbed such a matter of your own good that you choose not to rob others? Of course. What it cannot do is tell you *why it is important for you to be here to make that choice at all*. This is the problem with atheism – it can tell you what you should do, but not why you should be here to do it.

The atheist will tell you that it is better to be alive than dead. But they cannot actually know that, and they can provide you no reasoning why you should believe it either. It is **not** self-evident that the suffering of anyone simply because they are there to suffer is a good thing. And it is not reasonable to infer that continued living just because you are alive is good just by itself, either.

Like it or not, this war will be one by those who believe. Who believe that they personally are an important and valuable part of the universe, and tools in helping create the future that the good forces in the universe demand. The Muslims believe this and we do not. They are winning and we are not.

You must reconnect, you must look and see that the spiritual connection you have to the universe is of infinite value.   Then, you will have the power to reject the nonsense of the New Atheists and their Hard Left allies. You have to understand how badly the universe needs you, how badly your neighbors and friends and family need your contribution. How badly history is leaning on you to frame the next chapter of human existence.

I can give you some motivation; the Fermi Paradox. Despite our "calculations" – how they could ever reflect reality no one knows – it appears that we are the only advanced civilization in our part of the galaxy at least. It appears life is less common than we think, and advanced civilizations far more so.

I believe there are two ways that what intelligent life that has developed have self-destructed. The first is literally that, self destruction. They were not able to restrain their impulses and blew themselves up. The second way is the way we are doing it, allowing a less-advanced and less practical civilization take over.

Without future technological advances, the planet gets stuck using up their natural resources until they are gone, causing civilization to return to the stone age literally. I think this is a common fate of any planet with intelligent creatures.

So here we are slowly heading down that road ourselves. We are the only flickering candle of intelligence in our little corner of the universe, and if we do not protect it we will allow it to be snuffed out. But we have the chance to buck the trend, to do what it takes to protect our little flame and allow our people to advance and flourish. We're the only game in town, and we need to act like it. So connect yourself emotionally and psychologically to the importance of our existence and defend it.

We will fail as a species if you do not. There has to be an overwhelming sense of communion and unity with others if we are to save the lives of strangers. And that is what it takes, because saving a society or civilization is saving the lives of a lot of strangers whom you will never know. Yet you need to have a powerful enough connection to them and to your very life itself that the sacrifices you will need to make are done happily and voluntarily.

I only know we cannot fight back if we keep our hearts locked safely away in a jar in the china cabinet for safe keeping. We need all of you, and giving your all is a learned behavior motivated by the ability to love. You'll have to find a way to take your heart down off the shelf and use it like never before. Love may not be all we need, but we will get nowhere until we once again love others more than we love our own comfort.

It's the only way to make it happen for us. The only way to save ourselves.

SEVEN:
THE POWER OF DEATH AND LIFE

There is far, far too much made about the power of positive confession in the world. We are childish if we really believe it is our self-talk that makes us happy and successful. On the other hand, I believe it is far more important what we say to one another and how we say it. That is why the scripture I used as the title of this chapter says this power is in the tongue; it gives power and healing to others when spoken to them, not when spoken to yourself.

You do not have to say anything to yourself out loud for your mind to capture it; whatever you think is what you are. The tongue then is a tool to use for others, to encourage and motivate those around you to be better. There are so many instances where people who turn their lives around because they find someone who tells them, "I believe in you." This is more important than you could ever believe.

One of the greatest goods you can do is to expect the

best out of others, and express that you know they can live up to your expectations. The young especially respond to such a message more powerfully than anything else. No punishment or reward can do what the simple proclamation of belief can do. Humans can suffer what they must, and disrespect what they do not earn. But something magical seems to happen when we speak to who we believe they can be.

Accountability is the magic wand that has turned around the lives of millions of teenagers in America's inner cities and impoverished rural areas. It is up to us then to continue this practice and amplify it in our society. We have to end the practice of living up to other's low expectations.

What I am really talking about is the combination of public accountability and encouragement. Great schools, of which there are far too few in the West, know that kids respond greatly to being given real responsibility. We need to adapt this same idea on a much wider scale. We need to be convinced that we can and will be successful.

Not everybody is an actual thief, or a constant liar, or dishonorable or a fraud and a hypocrite. These are excuses used by those with less than good character for not improving their own personal state. They are not the charges made by those willing to look at themselves and try to be a better human being.

There are people in the world who are loyal and faithful. Many people really are patriotic, and honest, and honorable. Should we learn to hold each other to those standards, we might be able to fix the underlying weaknesses in our system of governance and daily life.

Let me give you some bad news; one way or another,

in the not-so-distant future, we are going to live in a much more traditional society than we do today. One of two different traditional societies. Either one we re-create for ourselves, or one we get from others, and that one is going to suck really badly. If we choose to reconstitute our own, we can all still be relatively happy. If we choose to fail, the other traditional society will have you attending Friday prayers at the Mosque, and if you refuse will cut your throat and leave you to bleed in the street, because that's what they do.

If we wish to survive and keep our freedom we will be required to change the way we speak about all of the things and persons we are engaged with as we go through our daily lives and attempt ourselves to contribute what we can to the common good. I hate to say it, but to a point propaganda works (depending on the person of course). We humans certainly respond to the things we are repeatedly told are true, else we would have no postmodernist movement and this book would not need to be written.

We need to change the way we speak and think about our nation and our civilization just as we did during the Cold War. We need to tell the story of the good as well as the bad, and we have to draw focus back on where we are right now, and the things that are happening in the world today and how we can fix it. I believe the Human Progress web site is an excellent place to start, as it gives us not the measure of history but of current conditions in the world.

Our enemies look at the past and speak of old crimes. We should look to the future and speak of current possibilities. Consistently, until it is our good voices that speak blessings win out over their hateful and greedy ones.

EIGHT:
WHO WANTS TO LIVE FOREVER

One of my favorite places in the whole world is Fort Rosecrans National Cemetery on the edge of the San Diego metro area. The cemetery itself is amazing, sitting high on the top of a ridge on a spit of land that encircles the San Diego Bay. Sitting on the high point of the ridge far above sea level and at the end of the peninsula, the views from Fort Rosecrans are incredible.

It is a place that is deeply peaceful and beautiful, and there are areas where you can get an amazing view of the San Diego Bay and the downtown of the city across the bay. One Sunday I was blessed with being able to watch a huge three masted schooner sail into the bay on a beautiful sunny day. It was breathtaking, and one of the most wonderful scenes I have ever personally seen.

That experience, in total, is a perfect representation of the other side. We live and survive in the mud, in the rain, through suffering and horrible pain. This leads us over time to believe the mud is all there is, unless you were lucky enough to be born into wealth or with special intelligence. And those things we go through in the mud and rain are common to all of us. But I have wonderful news for you; the sunny day is what awaits you on the other side if you will do life right. And I am not talking about heaven.

I am talking about the graves, the tombstones, the individual names engraved in the marble slabs with a simple cross on each one. And just like them, you too can be immortal even if you never become famous. There are levels to immortality. There is a common level to immortality available to us all, not just on a national hero/known level.

I was fortunate, my grandfather fought his way across North Africa, was transferred to England and part of the landing at Normandy. He was at the Battle of the Bulge, and described to me an encounter he had with an early version of napalm, which the Germans had not perfected. He recounted how he managed to strip off about eight layers of clothing, to have the last small piece fall to the frozen ground, still smoldering in the dirt. Had it hit him in warmer weather, he would have been dead.

My great uncle served as a cook for an airfield in the South Pacific, and he watched as early on in the Pacific theatre the American planes would be jumped as they attempted to land late in the day. The Japanese planes had longer range, so they would stay out of the way of the Allied planes then follow them back to their airfields and attack them when they were low on fuel. The Japanese rightly determined that any plane that fell from the sky was a win, even if it was not shot down. I am lucky, because these men gave me a sense of what value lies in the battle. There is a time and a place where and when it is important for those who will to rise up and strike a blow for right and for good. That time and place has a special name; today.

Consider it for a minute, and let me convince you. Great leaders are indeed remembered, but so are those with them. It was the Roman Legions that struck terror into their enemies, not just Caesar. The horse mounted cavalry of the Mongols drove the terrified peoples before them like chaff. The 300 Spartans likewise are remembered, though we do not know their individual names.

On and on I can go, those sacrificed at the Somme, the handful of pilots that stood up to Hitler during the blitz, the graves of those buried near Normandy. But it is not just military. It applies to other areas too. We do not know the names of all those who participated in putting a man on the moon, but they were each just as critical as Neil Armstrong to the success of that endeavor.

And believe it or not, though we do not know them directly, there are pictures of the control room and the crew in it at their desks, because we do give all credit. They are and will always be part of the story that is owned by all who participated in it as long as the American flag remains on the little satellite where it is planted.

And that is the nature of this truth, that those who were allies and comrades to the great conquests of life are also remembered if only indirectly. They also have medals and honor and the right to the quiet respect that all those who give everything to conquer are due. And should you be blessed enough to be wounded or even fall through you efforts, you are of all men most lucky. For you it shall be as Shakespeare speaks in Henry V:

"That he which hath no stomach to this fight,

Let him depart; his passport shall be made
And crowns for convoy put into his purse:
We would not die in that man's company
That fears his fellowship to die with us.
This day is called the feast of Crispian:
He that outlives this day, and comes safe home,
Will stand a tip-toe when the day is named,
And rouse him at the name of Crispian.
He that shall live this day, and see old age,
Will yearly on the vigil feast his neighbours,
And say 'To-morrow is Saint Crispian:'
Then will he strip his sleeve and show his scars.
And say 'These wounds I had on Crispin's day.'
Old men forget: yet all shall be forgot,
But he'll remember with advantages
What feats he did that day: then shall our names.
Familiar in his mouth as household words
Harry the king, Bedford and Exeter,
Warwick and Talbot, Salisbury and Gloucester,
Be in their flowing cups freshly remember'd."

And there is the truth, laid bare for you to see plainly, that those who participate are never fully forgotten, as we do not abandon our inventions and explorations and victories and accomplishments for the silliness of disagreement or delicate qualms. And even though all those names may not be on the lips of who look at the moon on a starry night, the fingerprints on that flag floating so far away through the night sky do not solely belong to Mr. Armstrong.

Everyone who took part in the efforts necessary to make that a flag a reality also have their thumbprints right there beside his. Every engineer who makes your iPad possible is just as vital as the man who started Apple, and the accomplishments that they made cannot be taken by the leader who could have not designed a single chip. You are not just putting in time, you are putting in yourself, and there in that place you also get a little piece of the ownership, recognized legally or not.

I do not know the families or neighbors of the men on the white marble markers covering Fort Rosecrans. Their individual stories are distant and unknown to me. It matters not. They did great exploits and rose from the mud and the rain to help turn back the dark clouds. And you too can rise up and do the same things in your time and in your ways, if you will just look for a battle to fight. It doesn't have to be military, just a war that needs won.

Give yourself to it, sacrifice for it, and one day you to will have a marker, a thing you leave the world which can never be taken from you. In this, you may well join that bright and shining row that across the centuries can still be heard the echo, "This is the way to meaning. This is the way to honor. Here lies the path to dignity and glory everlasting."

And you will have the rights equal to all those old men who march in musty uniforms on summer days that we may thank them for the peace they earned us. Sell your soul to the history we make every today, and this day you can begin to earn the one thing that can be taken from you; that you chose to matter.

Do not miss this great and wonderful path. It is part of your salvation, and you are wise in doubting your own value should you choose to turn away.

NINE:
THE GLORY OF SUFFERING

They were whipped, and they knew it. The British soldiers retreating towards the beaches of Dunkirk were simply trying to get home alive. Through daring and bold new tactics, the Germans had pierced the Belgian defenses, then turned the British lines in a matter of days. The Allied plan to do as they had before, rushing forward to protect Belgium and absorb the blow before the German army reached France had turned into a trap.

But Hitler had other ideas. He saw Britain as a future ally, and so he let the British and French troops slip away. He offered peace, then paused when the offer was rejected. He frittered away all of May while the Wehrmacht mopped up the few troops left in France. Likewise June was wasted on planning that should he have been serious about ending the war should already have been completed the previous year when Poland was invaded.

It was time desperately needed to prepare what defenses were available; the stout troops of the BEF, underequipped to the point many of them drilled with broomsticks and the quality British navy. Besides that, there were a few aircraft, mostly antiquated Typhoons along with a handful of new Spitfires. Pilots were in short supply, and by the end of the battle over Britain the pilot shortage reached the breaking point.

In July the Luftwaffe came in force. They made many strategic and tactical errors. The German fighters could barely fight for 30 minutes over London due to small fuel tanks. They had no heavy bombers, and the most common medium bomber they had was designed years earlier, and was out of date.

Their new longer range fighter, the ME 210 was a failure as a bomber escort, and required fighter cover itself. The whole battle could have been a forgone conclusion. But the Germans had some advantages and learned as they went. They had far larger numbers – they would get shot down at a rate of about 2:1 yet never ran short of aircraft and the losses were not severe.

They were wise enough to focus on bombing the British airfields in southern England, damaging the landing strips and the facilities at the airfields. They hit the factory that made the Spitfire engines in Portsmouth. They would send out flights of fighters without bombers, just to engage the British fighters freely, then send the bombers in when the RAF planes were short on fuel.

This went on for two full grueling months. Eventually every airfield took considerable damage, some being knocked out for a day or two at a time. The most forward radar station was taken out at one point. Yet still they came, desperately trying to press home their advantage.

They nearly did.

By September, the strain was starting to show. British fighter pilots were usually flying two missions a day. They were short on sleep. New pilots were not adequately prepared for combat, and were shot down at a faster rate than the pilots they replaced. It looked grim, and it was grim.

But eventually, the tide changed. September also brought changes in the British weather. An accidental dropping of bombs on Berlin infuriated Hitler, who ordered the bombers to attack London at night, and blast it to the ground. It was a close shave, probably more than we will ever know, but due to the courage of a couple hundred or so British pilots Western civilization would be preserved, at least for the moment.

The war itself would grind on for five more long years. Stalin would have his own scare the following summer, but in the West we can credit the incredible courage of Churchill and the pilots of the RAF for holding off the evil of the NAZI regime and give freedom a little breathing room. Churchill famously said, "Never was so much owed by so many to so few".

During the winter, the British people would be constantly bombarded by the Luftwaffe as they attacked the cities of the UK in order to spread terror and demoralize the nation. But here, the Germans lost. Courage is a funny thing; once someone has seen it in another, they often find it in themselves, too.

And so they did. Every night, they took to the subways to sleep, sending their children into the countryside out of harm's way. They cleared the rubble, and kept the faith.

They suffered the reverses of 1940 and 1941 in North Africa and Asia with resolve. Something rose up in them, made them determined to hold on. Churchill, chomping on his cigar became an image of the British bulldog mentality. In 1944, they faced the "Baby Blitz", then the bombardment of the V-1 and after that the V-2.

But these were small scale, and by then the war had turned. The Allies were beginning to close in on Hitler. The Japanese were turned back in India and the Pacific. Freedom would live on for a while longer, all because of the courage of a few.

This small history lesson was provided to give you the last encouragement I have to offer; that while sometimes suffering is necessary, it comes with it's own special reciprocal power. It turns out that suffering adds value to our deeds, turning doing good, our duty, into something special. Something remembered.

And here's the amazing thing about that, *there is no other kind of suffering*. All suffering of every type is an opportunity to courage, and courage turns doing good into something truly special. It has become a tradition that when a child beats cancer, they get to ring a ship's type bell to celebrate their victory. Because when you have courage in the face of suffering **you are something special.**

Is the suffering still bad? Oh, yeah. But it cannot have the last word without your permission. Will it get better? Maybe, it depends on the source of your ills. But no matter what it is, or whether or not you get relief, **you get the last word.** You get to say if it defeats you. You get to say if it poisons your mind. You get to say how you are going to respond.

You get to take the sharp sword of courage and slay all that will have power over you, for if suffering cannot be your master nothing will. Suffering is the last, deepest, blackest pit of the enemy, and at the same time a golden doorway to a better you and a better future, as beyond the horror of suffering the quiver of our enemy is spent. That's all there is.

So should you show the power to take life's worst and respond with your best, then you are indeed a hero to all those in this life and beyond who look at you and behold in that act the very form of God. All the good that you do from your place of suffering is etched into the history of the universe forever, and cannot be erased. Your resistance shall be duly noted by all those who see you and honored for what it is, even if they never say so out loud.

This is to be like God; not to create, but to take chaos and pain and from it make value and meaning. It is to literally subdue the earth. If not the earth around you at least the earth from which you are made. Suffering may be the sharpest arrow, but it remains so for the wicked and righteous alike.

It is also a cup from which we will all drink the sour flow of death one day. But he who overcomes will go with great comfort to that final rest. And we will still prove the value of that courage, for we move the needle of life the most when suffering is our tool.

So don't be afraid; if you will stand you cannot fall, and you will give lie to our fears that we are insignificant and empty beings filled with only greed and envy. Stand tall, and allow the life you were given to be your ally and not your foe. Stand tall, and allow all to see that our misery is but a shallow and frail creature that cannot pierce our hearts.

Stand tall and allow everyone to see what a mockery is the spirit of fear, for where faith is fear must flee. Believe in all that you are when you sacrifice, and that whatever you give will be returned a thousand-fold in honor and glory.

And now, go stand and take your rightful place among your fellow heroes.

Godspeed.

ABOUT THE AUTHOR

Thomas Spriggs has lived in the Phoenix metro for an interminable number of years. He is an award-winning graduate of the Walter Cronkite School of Journalism. He is currently an explorer, apprentice musician and fan of Jordan Peterson.
And as always, delightfully crabby.

www.ingramcontent.com/pod-product-compliance
Lightning Source LLC
Chambersburg PA
CBHW051223250726
48655CB00006B/2569